Sharp writing for smart people

Welcome to *AMAZING YOU – NUMEROLOGY*

Using numerology to reveal your destiny and the fascinating story of you is only part of the *Amazing You* series.

Astrology and *Spells* are available now with more coming soon. Read them and amaze your friends with your spellbinding talents.

BITE HERE!

Wanna join the gang? All the latest news, gossip and prize giveaways from BITE! **PLUS** more information on new titles in the *Amazing You* series.

Sign up NOW to join the BITE gang, and get a limited edition denim BITE bag or an exclusive preview copy of a brand new teen title, long before it's available in the shops.

To sign up text NUMBERS to 60022

or go to **www.bookswithbite.co.uk**

FREE! Text your full name (including middle name) to 60022 and we'll tell you the hidden meaning in your name and mobile number!

About the series

Amazing You is our stunning new Mind Body Spirit series. It shows you how to make the most of your life and boost your chances of success and happiness. You'll discover some fantastic things about you and your friends by trying out the great tips and fun exercises. See for yourself just how amazing you can be!

Available now
Astrology
Numerology
Spells

Coming soon
Crystals
Dreams
Face and Hand Reading
Fortune Telling
Graphology
Psychic Powers

Acknowledgements

My thanks to the hundreds of children and young adults I've talked to over the years. Your curiosity, freshness and insight were my inspiration while writing this book. A big thank you to my editor, Anne Clark, for her encouragement and positive energy. Many thanks to everyone at Hodder Children's Books for making this project happen, in particular Katie Sergeant for her help and support. And finally, many thanks to my partner Ray and my children, Robert and Ruth, for their love, enthusiasm and patience while I went into exile to complete this project.

About the author

Theresa Cheung was born into a family of psychics, astrologers and numerologists. She gave her first public numerology reading at the age of fourteen, and has been involved in the serious study of numerology for over twenty years. As a former English secondary school teacher and health and fitness instructor Theresa has worked with many young adults. She contributes regularly to women's magazines, such as *Red*, *She* and *Here's Health*, and is the author of over twenty health, popular psychology, humour and New Age books including *Dreams* and *Face and Hand Reading* in the *Amazing You* series.

Contents

123
456
789

Introduction

Trying to make sense of your life? Wondering what the future holds? Who doesn't? There are many ways to seek wisdom but numerology has to be one of the most intriguing, accurate and easy to use.

I first discovered numerology when I was thirteen and I haven't looked back since. Over the years I have used the guidance of this ancient knowledge to change my life in positive ways. The accuracy of numbers in my life and those close to me has been astonishing. I know how well numerology works – it's an amazing source of wisdom and a wonderful self-help tool – but I'll let you be the judge of that as you try it for yourself.

It's all in the numbers, so why not make numerology the secret code that only you and your friends understand? Read on. Count up your opportunities and unlock the secrets of success and happiness.

CHAPTER ONE

How it all adds up

Do you have a favourite number? Do numbers sometimes pop into your mind for no reason? Ever wondered why we say things like 'dressed to the nines', 'all at sixes and sevens', 'I've got your number', or 'he's number one'? Ever wondered why a cat has nine lives? (Why not two or four?) Why we cheer three times and why thirteen is considered unlucky?

There is a reason. Numbers have hidden meanings. Think about it. Your life is made up of numbers, from the day you were born to the number of your mobile phone. Although you don't know it yet, these numbers tell the story of your journey through life. And once you crack their secret code, numbers can help you make the most of your life and be the best that you can be.

What is numerology?

Numerology. Sounds like hard work. I'm no good at maths, so it's not for me.
    Sarah, 13

Let's get one thing straight before we begin.
Numerology isn't about maths. So relax. Yes,
there is some simple addition and subtraction
to do, but that's about as tough as it gets.
Numerology is the study of numbers and the
magical way they reveal things about YOU –
both the secret you and the you that everyone
sees. This book will show you that you really
can understand yourself and your life better by
working with the numbers in it.

123
456
789

✶ HOW DOES IT WORK?

Do numbers have magical power? It all sounds a bit strange to me.

Tania, 14

Let's get another thing straight. Numbers don't have magical power over you. Yet you must have realized by now that there is more at work in your life than just what you see – thoughts, feelings, energy, vibes. Ever heard of feng shui? The principles of feng shui give you the ability to change the energy in your home and thereby change your life. In the same way, numerology can help you work with the energy in your life and change it. Why? Because numbers carry certain energy and once you know your numbers and their hidden meanings, you have a secret code to help you change the energy in your life for the better.

3

Not so long ago

Although numerology probably has its origins in ancient Babylonia, and many different numerology systems have been used in different parts of the world, numerology is often associated with the sixth-century BC Greek mathematician and philosopher, Pythagoras. Pythagoras based his system on the belief that numbers were the source of energy in the world and that the numbers 1 through to 9 represented the nine stages of life. Centuries ago Pythagoras used the symbolic wisdom of numbers to help people understand themselves better, and it's much the same today. Numerology was and is still an important tool for understanding and self-knowledge.

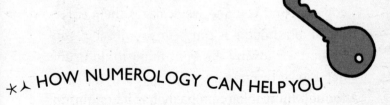

HOW NUMEROLOGY CAN HELP YOU

I don't get it. It's just numbers, isn't it? How can they tell me anything?
Chloe, 12

All numbers are significant, and numerologists believe that you can improve your chances of happiness and success by understanding the numbers influencing different areas of your life. The energy created by the number of your house, for instance, will influence the experience of all those living and working in it; your telephone number will attract certain situations; and the number of your birthday will bring certain strengths and challenges. The start date of a new job, the first date of a relationship, the name and number of your boyfriend and your friends – all can give you crucial clues about possible pitfalls and potential outcomes.

5

Numerology can also help you understand the people around you and what makes them tick. Best of all, though, it can help you develop your intuition – knowing the right thing to do or the right choice to make even when you don't know how or why you know – so that you can turn every situation, even negative ones, to your advantage.

⋆⅄ HOW TO USE THIS BOOK

To crack the secret code, grab this book, a pen and paper, and have ready your birth date and your full birth name. You can read this book from cover to cover, or you can dive right in to the chapters that are relevant to you. But I'm sure that once you have read about the numbers most applicable to you, you will want to find out more about the others. The more you know, the more you grow.

In the chapters that follow, you'll learn about

your birthday number, your personality number, your soul number, your life path number, and your destiny number, and you'll find out how you can apply numerology to your daily life. But don't go overboard with it all. Numerology can bring great insight but the most important tools you have will always be your intuition and your common sense. Numbers don't have any power over you. Ultimately you know best and you control your destiny. Okay, now that we've done the introductory stuff, let's take a deep breath and plunge right in with the most complex and fascinating of subjects: YOU.

123
456
789

CHAPTER TWO

YOU

Let's start with your birthday number. This number shows the way YOU approach life. It's simply the day you were born, whether that is the 1st or the 31st of the month. While it is not the most significant number in numerology, it's fun, easy to find and a good way to get you thinking along the right lines.

The only thing you need to bear in mind is that if your birthday is a two-digit number, anything from 10 to 31, you need to reduce that number to a single digit. You do this by adding together the two digits. For example, if you were born on the 16th of the month, you simply add 1 and 6, giving you a birthday number of 7. If you were born on the 27th, you simply add 2 and 7, giving you a birthday number of 9. The chart on page 10 will make things really simple:

1 If you were born on the 1st, 10th, 19th, 28th
your birthday number is 1.

2 If you were born on the 2nd, 11th, 20th, 29th
your birthday number is 2.

3 If you were born on the 3rd, 12th, 21st, 30th
your birthday number is 3.

4 If you were born on the 4th, 13th, 22nd, 31st
your birthday number is 4.

5 If you were born on the 5th, 14th, 23rd
your birthday number is 5.

6 If you were born on the 6th, 15th, 24th
your birthday number is 6.

7 If you were born on the 7th, 16th, 25th
your birthday number is 7.

8 If you were born on the 8th, 17th, 26th
your birthday number is 8.

9 If you were born on the 9th, 18th, 27th
your birthday number is 9.

The birthday number reflects what makes you unique, but it also shows what you have in common with other people who were born on the same day or have the same birthday number. After you have read the following descriptions, have some fun and work out who you know that has the same birthday number as you. Then think about how knowing your own birthday number and the birthday number of your friends and family can help you understand yourself and them better. (Why not include a friend's birthday number description with their next birthday card?)

As you read the descriptions remember that each number has a downside as well as an upside. Don't panic! The downside suggests challenges associated with a particular number, and just becoming aware of them can help you recognize, overcome and avoid them. Remember, you're the one in charge here. Numbers don't have any power over you. The power to choose a positive or a negative approach to life is within YOU and only YOU.

☆ ☆ ☆ *Birthday number 1:*

You are original and independent and have bags
of courage. You can easily stand up in front of
the class or put yourself forward for things that
would make others feel anxious. You are focused,
dynamic, creative, self-motivated and self-reliant.
You have lots of energy, and it's important for
you to keep active, mentally and physically. You
don't mind schoolwork as long as it challenges
you, and aerobics, jogging, cycling and swimming
are some of the many activities and sports you
may enjoy. You are a forger of fashion, often the
first off the mark with new trends, but because of
an indecisive streak you often buy things you
never wear.

Downside: Because you seem so confident, you
might come across as aloof and superior, which
can intimidate others and make you feel lonely.
Stop now and have a think about how interested
you are in other people. When you are with your
friends, what do you like to talk about the most –
yourself or what your friends are thinking and
feeling? You may also hesitate too long before

making decisions. This indecision can cause stress and anxiety-related illnesses such as bouts of indigestion, headaches and fatigue. Are you the kind of person who worries and makes excuses, or do you enjoy new situations and have the courage to seize opportunities? If you are the former, success and recognition will slip through your fingers until you find the will and energy to stop dithering, take some risks and get on with your life. The only way to learn and grow and have fun is to make mistakes. So forget perfect – perfect is impossible and boring.

Famous birthday 1s: Princess Diana, Julia Roberts, Missy Elliott, Kylie Minogue.

☆ ☆ ☆ *Birthday number 2:*

You are considerate and kind and a rock for others to lean on. Making decisions isn't a problem for you. You have patience and are good at weighing the pros and cons of situations and acting in everyone's best interests, not just your own. Friends love to hang around with you; you

value their opinions and want them to share all
the fun and excitement. You may be attracted to
anything that is connected with water, such as
swimming or water sports, as water is a calming
influence for you. You may also enjoy exercises
that are gentle, powerful and calming, like yoga.
You might like cooking, gardening and anything
that you feel makes the world a more beautiful
place. Your wardrobe may be understated, and
you tend to prefer neutral styles and trusty black
and white. But if you can be bold and invest in
some stronger colours and unusual styles, you'll
be surprised at the confidence they give you.

Downside: Rejection is your biggest fear, and this
can make you a bit nervous and at times overly
cautious and dependent on others. You may find
yourself easily hurt, and the remedy is to try not
to take things so personally. You may also be
inclined to take on the feelings of friends and
family. For example, you feel the hurt, confusion
and pain of your best friend when she breaks up
with her unfaithful boyfriend. You need to be
careful here. Too many emotional ups and downs
can influence your health and make you prone to

depression, skin allergies or nervous system complaints. Try to calm down and keep a sense of proportion. You can also be a bit dreamy and prone to mood swings. Watch out too for laziness and lack of motivation. For example, if you have an exam ahead and don't do any work, how can you expect to excel? Finding a balance between work and rest is essential for you.

Famous birthday 2s: Nicole Kidman, Jennifer Aniston, Britney Spears, David Beckham.

☆☆☆ *Birthday number 3:*

You are the creative one. In fact, you have to be creative, or you feel unhappy and unfulfilled. You love to be on the go and enjoy travelling to new places. You have a sense of fun, and your energy is contagious. You are bubbly, extrovert and a real tonic because you can make people laugh – the typical life of the party. You are smooth-talking, confident and so happy-go-lucky that you can get on well with almost everyone. You are one of life's optimists and make the most of every day, even bad ones, always finding something to smile about. You may be an avid reader, particularly of magazines that are full of real-life stories and useful bits of information. Art, or anything that gives you a chance to express yourself, holds a special place in your heart. As far as fashion is concerned, you love experimenting with different styles.

Downside: You may be so easygoing that you don't pay attention to the details of life, and this can lead to confusion and sloppiness. For instance, at times you may be too carefree with your diet and may eat or exercise too much. You can be scatterbrained and chaotic, and this can lead to speaking or doing something before you think and regretting it later. Because you have so many friends and interests you may sometimes feel quite unsure about who you like to spend time with and what you enjoy doing. Instead of being Ms Popular and a Jill-of-all-trades, try to focus more on what is really important and the people you really care about.

Famous birthday 3s: Charlotte Church, Celine Dion, Prince William, Tom Cruise.

☆☆☆ *Birthday number 4:*

Rather like the tortoise who 'raced' the hare and eventually won, the birthday number 4 understands that hard work, discipline and perseverance are often the reasons for success. Even though you wouldn't dream of telling your friends, you do actually like working hard because it gives you a sense of satisfaction that you have achieved something at the end of the day. And because you like to think you have earned the right to a good grade, a great date or good health. Indeed, you generally put a lot of effort into all areas of your life – school, relationships, health – to make it all run smoothly. Security is an important need for you, and you are a loyal and dependable friend who never loses sight of the needs of others. You tend to be practical, grounded and generally organized. If you say you are going to do something, you do it to the best of your ability, making you a very focused and special person. Strenuous exercise may not appeal and you may prefer gentler activities, such as walking, swimming, reading, chatting to friends or chilling out in front of the television. You feel happiest in your jeans and are a firm believer in inner over outer beauty. You probably don't know your Prada from your Calvin Klein.

Downside: There is a tendency to go the other way and spend a lot of your time thinking about material things at the expense of other aspects of your life. You may also be so structured and disciplined that other people find it hard to get to know you. You dislike anything that upsets your routine because you are a creature of habit. Unfortunately, this rigidity may place too many restrictions on others so they feel suffocated. At times you may feel stifled by the routine and order of your life, and if you can't find anything to inspire you this can lead to laziness and lack of motivation.

Famous birthday 4s: J K Rowling, Minnie Driver, Robbie Williams, Justin Timberlake.

☆☆☆ *Birthday number 5:*

Change is the key word for birthday number 5s. You have a sense of adventure and a desire for constant excitement and stimulation. You are adaptable, daring, and progressive, and you love your freedom. Although you often act on impulse, you do also have a lot of common sense. For instance, if a friend tells you something, you like to check it out yourself. It's not that you don't trust your friend, it's just that you like to base your life on facts, not hearsay. This lovely combination of an adventurous spirit with level-headedness means that you are quick-witted and observant and you don't miss a trick. You are interested in what other people have to say and are as a result a popular person. You love meeting new people, and parties or Internet chat rooms – anywhere you can collect new information – are of particular interest to you. You live every day to the full and always give it your best, which makes you an inspiring and fascinating person to know. Your fashion sense is as lively as you are. You live for labels and wouldn't put the rubbish out looking less than your best.

Downside: Number 5 birthdays sometimes find it hard to bond with people as they are forever flitting in and out of others' lives. Perhaps you sometimes feel as if you don't know who you are, where you want to go and who you want to be with. This lack of direction may lead to lack of discipline. Alternatively, you may be so disciplined that you restrict yourself too much. For example, you make a chocolate cake but don't allow yourself to have any. You can be fickle and find it hard to settle down, get your work done and stay in one place for more than a few minutes. But if you can find the discipline and staying power you have the ability to do anything you put your mind to.

Famous birthday 5s: Kate Winslet, Ralph Lauren, Halle Berry, William Shakespeare.

☆ ☆ ☆ *Birthday number 6:*

Birthday number 6s like to experience the best that life has to offer, so designer brands and the latest fashion in accessories, clothes and food are usually a must. You love marathon shopping trips, which you find both absorbing and relaxing. You take great pride in the way you look. Life tends to revolve around your home and your closest friends, and you are very caring towards your friends and family. If anything should upset them you take on their problems as if they were your own and do all you can to help them. You are extremely sensitive towards others and seem to always know instinctively when to help and when to give them space, which makes you the ideal friend. You enjoy giving and may devote time to helping others and serving the community.

Downside: Your obsession with appearance, or making your home environment beautifully perfect, could mean that you end up neglecting important things in life, like school, and your friends may find it hard to relax when you are around. Sixes are vulnerable to stress-related aches and pains, so it is crucial for you to find more time to just relax and chill out. You may also get overinvolved in the problems of family and friends. Learning tolerance and respect for the needs and wishes of others could prove crucial for your happiness and for the happiness of those around you.

Famous birthday 6s: JLo, Sarah Ferguson, Prince Harry, George Clooney.

☆☆☆ *Birthday number 7:*

You are a deep thinker who likes to ponder situations – sometimes for so long that you forget to be somewhere on time. The arts are of strong interest to you, and you are motivated to seek answers to the mysteries of life. You like to be inspired, and you enjoy a challenge. You are sensitive to other people's needs and enjoy reading, meditation, classical music, ballet or opera and like to spend lots of time on your own to recharge your batteries. You particularly like nature walks, woods, gardens and rivers, spending as much time in nature as possible. You love and respect those close to you, but you like to choose when you see them. You find fashion frustrating, and although you know what's hot and what's not, you may not care to experiment.

22

Downside: You have a tendency to be dreamy and detached from life, sometimes so much so that you feel lonely. At times you can feel so vulnerable that you isolate yourself from life instead of experiencing it, but the only way for you to feel emotionally strong is to limit the time you spend alone and reconnect with your friends and family. Remind yourself that letting others know what you think and feel is a sign not of weakness but of strength. You may be prone to fatigue and overly concerned with your health so that you notice every little spot and sneeze. Try to relax a bit more and find a sense of perspective, not just as far as your health is concerned but in all areas of your life.

Famous birthday 7s: Anna Kournikova, Will Smith, Catherine Zeta-Jones, Madonna.

☆☆☆ *Birthday number 8:*

The chances are you are hardworking and thorough, and a natural leader. In addition, you are ambitious and have a need for material success and security. You move through life with clearly defined goals and are very much your own person. You may even enjoy obstacles, as you see them not as a sign of rejection but as a natural part of life, and they drive you harder towards success. You have charisma and are generally a popular person. You enjoy other people's company but are just as happy on your own. The number 8 also brings with it the responsibility of helping others, and people will tend to rely on you for support, which you freely give. You love to be active and particularly enjoy exercise that focuses your mind and strengthens your body, such as working out in the gym, running or horse riding. You may also have a tendency to spend money on things you don't really need. Be honest, now: how many pairs of shoes do you own that you just can't walk in?

Downside: Number 8s like to be winners, and you might hog the limelight because you crave recognition. You may be an incredible exhibitionist and could be known for your mistakes more than for your successes. When your confidence is low you can be demanding and inflexible and can come across as arrogant. You may also give up too easily when the going gets tough, allowing others to pull you in directions that you aren't sure you want to go in. Finding a balance between activity and non-activity may be an area of concern and could influence your health.

Famous birthday 8s: Eminem, Sandra Bullock, Elvis, Kevin Spacey.

☆☆☆ *Birthday number 9:*

You are generous, passionate, sensitive and concerned for the planet you live on. Your interests run in every direction, and you are very talented. Really, there is nothing you couldn't do if you set your mind to it. You also never take for granted what you already have and always have a kind or witty word when friends feel low. Despite not always being sure which direction you want your life to go in, you are a very strong person. This strength comes from your unshakeable belief that life will guide you to the path that is right for you and that things will always work out for the best. You love to curl up in front of the television for relaxation, but you are just as happy at parties and social events. Best of all, though, you love to let off steam by gossiping with your friends in cafés. With your creative flair you are queen of your own style when it comes to fashion and quick to adapt to new trends to suit you.

Downside: Be careful, number 9s, that you don't start to think that your opinions are the only correct ones. There's a word for that, and it's 'arrogant'. Paradoxically, you may keep your feelings too much to yourself because you fear that you won't be liked. This approach to life only works in the short term. In the long term it leads to anger, resentment, unpredictable behaviour and emotional outbursts when you can't keep your feelings to yourself anymore. Try not to have ridiculously high expectations of yourself and others. Life isn't perfect, and it isn't meant to be. Watch out that you don't neglect your health or get too self-indulgent.

Famous birthday 9s: Avril Lavigne, Christina Aguilera, Brad Pitt, Hugh Grant.

✶⅄ YOUR SPECIAL DAY

What did you think about your birthday number? Did some of it ring true? Did you learn something new about yourself?

If you didn't feel connected to the comments under your birthday number, don't toss this book away. You are just beginning your life, and the qualities outlined may not have developed in you yet. Also bear in mind that most numerologists don't consider the birthday number to be as revealing or as insightful as your personality, soul, life path and destiny numbers, which we will figure out in the next few chapters. We started with the birthday number because it's the easiest and most obvious. So hang in there if you aren't convinced yet.

And never forget as you read this book that you and only you have the power to change your life for the better. You control your destiny by the choices you make every day of your life. If you want something, find out what you need to do to get it. If you don't like something, do all that you can to change it. Think about the kind of person you want to be and what you want to achieve in your life. Numerology can help point you in the right direction, but it can't make the changes or choices for you. If you want to make a change in your life, the place to start is with yourself, not with your parents, your boyfriend, friends or your teacher. All change starts with YOU.

CHAPTER THREE

Friendship

When it comes to friendship knowing someone's personality number is a form of instant analysis that can help you read other people very quickly. It can help you gain insight into a friend's personality so that you can understand them better and get a sense of what motivates them. Once you know where your friends are coming from, you can connect and communicate with them better. And knowing your own personality number can also help make you a better friend by keeping you in touch with your own needs and showing you what you can do to help improve your friendships. Do bear in mind though that the personality number can't tell you everything. The most important things when it comes to forming friendships will always be your common sense and judgement.

Our personalities take on the shading of the people we hang around with. You must have felt this. If your best friend comes to school in a tearful mood, you tend to tone down your mood too. So how can you tell what someone's true personality is? Simply find out what their personality number is and get a glimpse into their character, for the personality number reveals someone when they are truly at ease and being themselves.

But before we find out all about your friends, let's find out about you. What's *your* personality number?

Find your personality number

To find your personality number, write out your first, middle (if there is one) and last name in full. Use the name you were given at birth – the one that appears on your birth certificate – even if you never use the whole thing. Why? Because that's the name that influences you throughout your whole life.

Then pick the consonants out of your name – that's any letter except a, e, i, o, u – and match each consonant with the number you find in the following chart. Then add all those numbers till they become a single digit.

B	2	K	2	S	1
C	3	L	3	T	2
D	4	M	4	V	4
F	6	N	5	W	5
G	7	P	7	X	6
H	8	Q	8	Y	7
J	1	R	9	Z	8

For example: CHLOE ANN SMITH =

C–3, H–8, L–3, N–5, N–5, S–1, M–4, T–2, H–8

Then add all the numbers up:

3 + 8 + 3 + 5 + 5 + 1 + 4 + 2 + 8 = 39

If you end up with a single-digit number, that's your personality number, but if you end up with a double-digit number, like Chloe's, add the two digits together until you have a single digit.

For example, 3 + 9 = 12. Once again we have a double digit, so we add the numbers together again. In Chloe's case 1 + 2 = 3. Chloe's personality number is 3.

Simple, isn't it?

Okay! Ready? It's time now to look at the typical traits for each number. Just by becoming aware of your personality number, you can make better decisions about how you respond, act and behave in social situations. For each number, have a think about the following two questions:

Do I feel comfortable with these traits?

Do I want to change the image I project to others?

Personality number 1:

✱ Impeccably dressed and ultra cool.

✱ Confident, appearing to need no-one.

✱ Has plenty of ambition and willpower.

✱ Likes to have everything their own way.

Inspiring and exciting qualities in a person? Or does the number 1 personality put off people by coming across as unapproachable or too forceful in social situations?

Personality number 2:

✱ Modest and reserved.

✱ A good listener.

✱ Doesn't tend to argue – can't stand conflict.

✱ Quiet, honest, charming and easygoing.

The ideal companion? Or can the number 2 personality appear too colourless and a potential doormat for others to wipe their feet on? Are your friendships supportive and intimate, or are you being overly dependent on others?

Personality number 3:

✱ Magnetic, fun personality – the life of the party.

✱ Great talker – enthusiastic, entertaining and charming.

✱ Expressive and intelligent with an optimistic outlook on life.

✱ Great sense of humour.

Sounds like a lot of fun – or does the tendency to exaggerate and entertain mean that others don't take you as seriously as you'd like?

Personality number 4:

✱ Shy and reserved at times.

✱ Hardworking, reliable and trustworthy.

✱ Responsible, independent and well balanced.

✱ The person others turn to when they are in trouble, since you provide a shoulder to cry on, help and support.

A tower of strength – or do you need to loosen up a bit and let go of the restrictions imposed by rigidity and stubbornness? Do you need to jazz up your life, your wardrobe, and your outlook?

Personality number 5:

� Likes change, movement and variety.

� A free spirit with a live-in-the-now attitude to life.

� Sparky, magnetic and witty personality.

� Outgoing and exuberant.

A real tonic – or is your happy-go-lucky approach sometimes a way of escaping the responsibilities of life or friendship? Is it time to stop wasting energy and try just a little stability?

Personality number 6:

✳ Idealist and perfectionist.

✳ Responsible and caring.

✳ Sympathetic and inspires confidence.

✳ Giving nature that loves to spread goodwill.

A natural-born teacher with the good of everyone at heart – or are you putting too much pressure on yourself and taking on too many problems that aren't your own thereby neglecting your own needs?

6

7

Personality number 7:

✳ Thoughtful and intelligent.

✳ Difficult to get close to, but once you get to know someone you make a fascinating and loyal friend.

✳ Refined and stylish.

✳ The state of the world saddens and angers you, but instead of distancing yourself from it you concern yourself with it.

Is your air of secrecy, independence and mystery intriguing – or does your aloof attitude make you feel lonely at times? Friendship needs a certain amount of emotional investment to make it work, and could your withdrawal sometimes come across as lack of interest?

Personality number 8:

�֍ Larger than life.

✱ Confident, intelligent and assertive.

✱ Good judge of character.

✱ Appears to be the one with authority.

Do you enjoy your power – or does your number 8 natural air of authority sometimes come across as cold, formal, controlling and tactless? Do you need to soften some of your traits a little so that people feel more comfortable around you?

Personality number 9:

9

* Generous, tolerant and compassionate.

* Warm, kind and caring.

* Emotional and vulnerable.

* Idealistic, honest and can't tolerate injustice.

Do you sometimes get overinvolved in other people's problems and find it hard to take the strain? Are you sensitive and aware, or do you take life a little too seriously? You may wear black a lot – why not add some lighter colours to your wardrobe to bring lighter moods?

⋆⅄ UNDERSTANDING YOUR FRIENDS

Now work out the personality numbers of your friends. Does it help you understand them a little better? For example, can you now understand:

* Why your personality number 1 friend loves to be in charge?

* Why your personality number 2 friend loves intimate chats about life, the universe and everything?

* Why your personality number 3 friend loves to gossip?

* Why your personality number 4 friend will always make sure her homework is a priority?

* Why your personality number 5 friend seems to know everybody?

* Why your personality number 6 friend always has an answer for everything?

* Why your personality number 8 friend longs to be famous?

* Why your personality number 7 and 9 friends always seem to have something on their mind?

☆↗ THERE'S MORE TO YOU THAN MEETS THE EYE

Now that you have had a think about your personality number and the personalities of your friends, remind yourself that your personality is the outer you that others see. Is there anything you might like to change about the way others see you? How does this fit in with your birthday number? Remember that your personality number is just one part of the unique pattern that makes up you. It may not be an adequate reflection of who you are. As you'll see in the next chapter, there is so much more to you than just your personality! Read on and find out!

CHAPTER FOUR

Love and relationships

There's this guy I really like. I want to ask him out, but he's a real mystery and quite hard to get to know. I can't figure out what he is all about.

Kelly, 13

Sometimes I just don't know where she is coming from. Everything I do seems to be wrong. I wish I could understand her. I hate all this arguing and game playing.

Terry, 17

In numerology your secret needs and desires are told in the soul number. It's not uncommon for people to learn their soul number and find that it reveals their heart's desire – what they long for, what really motivates them and what they need to feel happy. In this chapter you'll learn about your soul number and how knowing it can help you find or keep the perfect mate.

When it comes to close, heartfelt relationships, you'll want to look to the soul number. But before we get into soul mate stuff, let's find out how to calculate your soul number and see what it reveals about you.

Finding your soul number

Just like the personality number, your soul number is calculated from your full name at birth. Unlike the personality number, the soul number is found from the vowels in your name, which are the letters a, e, i, o, u. To reveal those all important secret desires hidden in your name, write down your name and give each vowel a number from the following chart. Add the numbers up.

A 1

E 5

I 9

O 6

U 3

Then, as before, add all the numbers up till you get to a single digit. For example: Linda Ann Price's soul number is 7.

L 1–9 N D A–1 A–1 N N P R 1–9 C E–5

9 + 1 + 1 + 9 + 5 = 25; add 2 +5 =

soul number 7

The soul number is what motivates you or what you seek within your heart. It is truly your heart's desire. So what makes your heart sing?

Soul number 1 needs to stand out from the crowd.

You don't like taking orders or being subordinate. Taking instructions from people in authority – teachers for example – won't be easy, and you'll feel much happier later in life when you have your independence. Although you long to break free and are ambitious, courageous and headstrong, you are sensible enough to bide your time and recognize that your priority right now is to nurture your talents at school or work and not squander your chances with pointless rebellion. On the downside, you can be selfish, arrogant and impatient as well as blunt, tactless and lacking in sensitivity. Clever, charming and independent, you expect your partner to be the same and can't stand neediness. An uncharacteristic lack of confidence often stops you going for what you want when it comes to relationships. Try harnessing the strength you know you have when it comes to affairs of the heart.

Soul number 2 needs peace and harmony.

You are a warm and loving soul and can bring great support and strength to others because you are a giver rather than a taker. The downside is that you tend to overreact to criticism and rejection and can be too keen to please. You sometimes give so much you forget to give to yourself, and you have to be careful you don't become too dependent or needy in relationships – it's a real turn-off. You are always happier in a couple than alone, and no-one makes a more loving companion than a person with a number 2 soul number. In love you are sensitive and supportive but often don't get what you give, so try being a bit more demanding in relationships.

Soul number 3 needs to inspire and create.

You want to make other people happy, to laugh and to encourage everyone to be the best that they can be. You are creative and love to express yourself and could have artistic talent. You enjoy socializing and have a great sense of humour and bags of enthusiasm. You are also romantic and very passionate in love. The downside is that you can be a terrible flirt and a real heartbreaker. You can change your mind (and your friends and/or boyfriend) from one moment to the next, but, hey, this isn't fickle, it's because you just want to have fun! You are an energetic and supportive partner, but your energy can sometimes be overwhelming. Also your tendency to gossip about intimate details can embarrass your boyfriend, so try to be more discreet.

Soul number 4 needs a goal to work towards.

You are hardworking, honest, practical and determined and operate best in an environment that is organized and disciplined. You aren't the kind of person to play games in relationships, and right from the start you like to know where you stand. In short, you like to know the score and be in control with as few surprises as possible along the way. In matters of the heart you are a caring, loving partner, but you aren't particularly romantic, preferring to give or receive practical gifts and have well-planned engagements. It's great that you are loyal and stable in your relationships, but the downside is that you can sometimes be narrow-minded, unimaginative and harsh.

Soul number 5 needs to break free.

You are a freedom lover. You don't like details and could have problems sticking to a routine or being on time. You have a passion for change and travel and can't stand to feel trapped. You are attractive, charismatic, a risk taker and very sexy. If you have a soul number 5 you should be careful not to seek change for change itself and need to guard against excess when it comes to partying. Though a good argument can keep passion alive, it can be hard going for your partner, and it takes its toll on the relationship in the long run. What if 5 is your sweetheart? Find ways to keep him interested or he won't be around for long.

Soul number 6 needs to be needed.

Home, family, harmony and beauty are dear to your heart. You can handle a lot of responsibility and have a natural healing ability. You are loyal, understanding and not afraid of commitment. You want to protect, nurture and support your loved ones. Your dearest wish is to find someone you can share your life with and build a home and family together. You are a loving and loyal partner but don't vocalize your feelings enough, and this can lead to feelings of resentment in the long run. The downside is that you can also be judgemental and unforgiving, and you may scare off potential friends and boyfriends by demanding commitment and devotion too soon with all those heavy 'where do I stand?' talks.

Soul number 7 needs time to think.

If you have 7 as your soul number you long for wisdom and knowledge. You really do like to be left alone – to read and to think. You like your environments to be quiet, and you love nature and the outdoors. You are very intuitive and can sense people's moods immediately. The downside is that you often only see things in your way. In love you may find it hard to open up since you are such a sensitive person, and relationships tend to be very private, one-to-one affairs, with little time for parties or socializing. Although you are an idealist at heart, your cynical side often takes over, and you may over-analyse relationships in a destructive way. Try to accept that you can't control life, and enjoy the ride.

Soul number 8 needs power and recognition.

With 8 for your soul number, you like to be the one in charge. You have good judgement and are efficient and hardworking. You have courage and strength of will, and you admire and seek power. You can be warm and loving, but making your mark on the world tends to take priority over close relationships. Take care that you don't get too material-minded and let work take over your life. You could end up feeling very alone. You are confident and feisty and quite open about your feelings, but you do need to be more aware of others' feelings, especially if they are less vocal about things than you are.

Soul number 9 needs to reform and improve.

You are independent and love to travel; you don't like being cooped up or fenced in. You are the very soul of love and compassion and strive for universal perfection. You are loving, idealistic and romantic and really believe that out there somewhere is a soul mate for each person. Deeply sensitive, you are often torn between your own needs and the needs of others. You are as idealistic about love as you are about life and need to find a more practical partner who can inject a dose of common sense into the relationship. The downside is that you can come across as a bit intense in your longing to be needed and loved.

Are you right for each other?

The importance of knowing what other people are 'within their hearts' cannot be stressed enough as far as love is concerned. Knowing someone's soul number can help you assess just how compatible you are. It can alert you to potential conflicts, and help you understand where the guy of your dreams is coming from.

I'd been with my boyfriend for about a year when I discovered numerology. We had fun together, but I wanted more. I was also scared to lose him by pressing for more commitment. When I found out his soul number was a 3 and I'm a 2, it all made sense.

Mia, 15

I thought my boyfriend wasn't that keen on me 'cause sometimes he seemed so distant. I stopped blaming myself when I found out that he's a soul number 7 and really needs space and time to himself.
Sophie, 16

Be careful not to judge anyone as good or bad, right or wrong. It is best to use numerology to understand other people, not judge them. If conflicting things appear – for example, you are very spiritual but your boyfriend or potential boyfriend is very material – it might be wise to remember that not only do opposites attract, they can sometimes be good for each other. What you need to think about is: are the goals of the person I'm interested in something that I want to be a part of? And at the end of the day don't take the soul number as the last word – like every other number in numerology you need to use what you learn in conjunction with your common sense.

Have a go now. Compare your soul number with the soul number of someone you are in a relationship with or have your eye on. If you want to know if your new love interest will be loyal, open-minded and sensitive to your needs, a 4, 6 or 9 might provide these qualities. If, on the other hand, you are looking for someone who will be supportive and loving, find a number 2. If you want excitement, look for a number 3 or 5. If you want someone assertive, look for a number 1 or 8. If you would like someone thoughtful and sincere, check out a number 7 or 9. As we have seen, every soul number has certain needs, and when you understand those needs you'll understand how compatible you'll be with a person who has that number.

✳⅄ FINDING YOUR SOUL MATE

If you and the person you're interested in have the same soul number, there can be a strong emotional tie. In fact, a matching pair of soul numbers suggests that you both want the same things, which could make for a strong bond between you.

But what if you find that your mate's soul number is different from yours? Naturally, you'll be wondering about compatibility. Don't feel disappointed. Remember, there is nothing like difference of opinion to keep a relationship alive.

The secret is in the difference – the mathematical difference between your numbers. For example, if you have a 4 soul number and your boyfriend has a 9, the difference between these numbers is 5 (9 - 4 = 5). So the key to resolving differences will be working together to honour the characteristics of number 5: change and a need for space without compromising the relationship. These are the traits you both want to work on so that your 4 soul can feel secure and your partner's 9 soul can fulfil his or her wish to express their humanitarian need to do good in the world.

Of course it will really help if you study the characteristics of each number so that you can gain valuable insight into your needs as well as your boyfriend's. For example if a 9 soul doesn't understand that security and stability are crucial for a number 4, then you won't experience compatibility. So what's the difference? Once you

know, you can use it to your
relationship's advantage.

* When 1 is the difference: Respect each
  other's independence and individuality.

* When 2 is the difference: Honour each other's
  sensitive points and work together.

* When 3 is the difference: Communicate
  honestly with each other and don't keep any
  emotions hidden.

* When 4 is the difference: Set good boundaries
  and maintain them with love and kindness.

* When 5 is the difference: Find a way to give
  each other that sense of freedom without
  compromising the relationship.

* When 6 is the difference: Stop being stubborn
  and restore a sense of balance with love,
  kindness and respect.

* When 7 is the difference: Respect your
  and your partner's needs to be alone,
  to have private time and space.

❋ When 8 is the difference: Power struggles could threaten your relationship, so work on softening your response to each other.

✢✤ YOUR SECRET TOOL

When it's not a love relationship you are thinking about but a relationship with a family member, friend or teacher, examining the other person's soul and personality numbers will give you a tremendous insight into what you can and can't expect from the relationship and what you can do to improve it. If you are looking for a close relationship, you'll want to look to your soul number, and if you are looking to get along with someone, the personality number is the one to check out. Should some of your numbers match, there will be a greater basis for understanding and sharing the same approach to life. If there are differences, refer to the differences chart to turn things to your advantage.

No-one really knows the secret formula for the perfect relationship. Love is and always will be a mystery. Numbers won't make someone fall in love with you, but they can help you find the best matches. The soul number is your secret tool when trying to date that special someone. It reveals thoughts, ambitions and desires of which a person is often unaware and helps you make smarter choices in your love life. Try it and see!

CHAPTER FIVE

Home and family

Numbers influence many areas of your life, and now we'll check out your house and telephone numbers. Your house number can tell you a great deal about the characteristics of your house and what goes on there. Why is it good to know this? Because knowing what energies influence your house can help you live more harmoniously and productively in it.

Figuring out your house number

It's easy to figure out your apartment or house number: just reduce the numbers of your house or apartment to a single digit. For example 135, Staines Road would have a house number of 1 + 3 + 5 = 9. This would be a home for the compassionate and tolerant, and for it to be a happy home individual feelings must be respected.

If you live in a named house, work out the letter number equivalents and reduce them to a single digit. Also, if your house number has an A, B or C after the number, for example, Flat 3B, add the number equivalent to the letter, which in this case would be 2, making the total house number 5.

Letters and their numbers

A	1		J	1		S	1
B	2		K	2		T	2
C	3		L	3		U	3
D	4		M	4		V	4
E	5		N	5		W	5
F	6		O	6		X	6
G	7		P	7		Y	7
H	8		Q	8		Z	8
I	9		R	9			

Place names

Some numerologists believe that a street or even a country's name has significance. Check out this list of country names and numbers and see if you agree.

Britain 1 (stands alone)

Australia 3 (friendly)

America 5 (freedom loving)

Japan 6 (duty and family)

Now try it on your own town or village.

MEANINGS OF HOUSE NUMBERS

The number 1 house:

This is a house for independent, self-reliant people. It will encourage individuality,

61

determination and creativity. The challenge of this house is that you may feel isolated or alone if you are the dependent type. And if you are independent there could be power struggles.

The number 2 house:

Typically a quiet house where patience, sensitivity and gentleness thrive. A willingness to cooperate is crucial. It's not a good house for someone who wants to be alone. The challenge of this house is that any form of conflict or discord will be exaggerated out of all proportion, and there may be too much attention to nitpicking detail rather than to what really matters.

The number 3 house:

A fun house where you can feel positive because enthusiasm and charm abound. There is a lot of room for creative expression here. However, the number 3 house is rather excitable and often crammed with too many guests and friends, which can lead to creative chaos. You need to be lighthearted to live here.

The number 4 house:

This is the house if you want security and stability. It is a house that demands order and economy and is a haven for those who aren't afraid of hard work and discipline. However, there is a tendency to be too rigid and inflexible, so the number 4 house might need to find ways to loosen up.

The number 5 house:

The 5 house is one of movement and change. It's a hub of activity, and change is constant with little emphasis on routine. Variety is the norm, and life is never dull. The challenge here is that there may be too many comings and goings, and it may be hard to feel rested in this house.

The number 6 house:

Love of children, pets, animals and family traditions are classic for the number 6 house. It is a warm, caring and nurturing environment. If you hate duty and responsibility this could cause tension within this peaceful home.

The number 7 house:

The 7 house is a retreat for those who need to rest and recuperate from the busy world. It's perfect for those who like to spend time alone. If you like to entertain and have friends round regularly, then this may not be the ideal house for you.

The number 8 house:

The 8 house tends to be a place of hard work or business activity. The number 8 brings recognition and respect from the community. Success is attracted to this house. The challenge is that this house incurs big expenses. Careful management of money, honesty and integrity is called for.

The number 9 house:

This is the home for the compassionate and the tolerant. If you have a burning desire to help the world, this is the house number for you. You'll find people drawn to you for your humanitarian outlook, your compassion and your wisdom. However, individual feelings can sometimes be hidden behind the greater good, and this can lead to resentment and passionate outpourings of emotion.

Does your phone number ring true?

As with other numbers in your life, your phone number and mobile phone number have meanings that should not be ignored. Checking out the meaning of the number reveals what this phone number may bring. When figuring out your phone number, forget the area code or general code, as its effect is too general, and only use the last six digits to calculate the phone number meaning. For example, if your phone number is 07808 180326 simply add 1 + 8 + 0 + 3 + 2 + 6, which totals 20, and reduce to a single digit, in this case 2 (2 + 0 = 2). The number 2 is all about listening and being supportive, so with a number 2 telephone number you'll find that lots of friends call you for advice and support. Why not have a go now and see what numerological message your phone is giving you and sending out to those who call? Use the following chart for handy reference, and see how you can work with the energy of your phone number.

1: Beginnings, independence, motivation, leadership, strength.

2: Harmony, relationships, support, unity, cooperation.

3: Honesty, imagination, optimism, creativity, happiness.

4: Discipline, responsibility, security, hard work, seriousness.

5: Change, versatility, excitement, freedom.

6: Balance, nurturing, duty, family focus, responsibility.

7: Wisdom, thoughtfulness, solitude, spiritual focus, mystery.

8: Authority, power, success, material wealth.

9: Transformation, global awareness, perfection, vision.

Hopefully by now you're becoming more aware of the numbers in your life. At all times you're the one in charge and numbers shouldn't take over your life but try not to take for granted the hidden meanings and important secrets of the significant numbers in your life. Use them to understand yourself, the people you care about and what unique message you are sending out to the world.

CHAPTER SIX

School, work and money

All my friends seem to know what they want to study and do with their lives. I haven't a clue. I wish I knew what I could be good at. That would be a starting point.

Kylie, 12

Your life path number is your own unique path in life and is the place to look when seeking guidance about school and work. It can be used to indicate positive study and work options. It tells of areas in which you may excel even without training. In short, it tells you what you were born to be!

Your life path number is calculated by adding up the numbers in your day, month and year of birth. Here's how to calculate your life path number if you were born on 9th November 1991:

9 (day) + 1 + 1 (month) + 1 + 9 + 9 + 1 (year) =
31

3 + 1 = 4
Your life path number is 4.

So write down your date of birth, do the sums
and refer to the following info.

*⋆

Life path number 1:

Most important for you right now is to learn to
stand on your own two feet, and this means
working hard at school without having to be
prompted because you know it is the best way to
increase your chances of success in life. Once you
do seize the initiative in your life you are ready to
move to the next level – leadership.

You are a born leader, and you may already
have held positions of responsibility at school or
at home. You may find it hard to be told what to
do by parents and teachers and won't feel truly
fulfilled until you leave school and strike out on
your own. Make sure, though, that you hang in
there until you have the knowledge and skills you

need to succeed. Your career options are many and varied, as you could excel in any job that allows you to take the lead and express your individuality. Look for study or work that allows you to use your quick wits, such as the entertainment industry, government, business or health.

★ ★

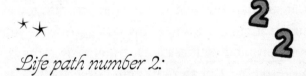

Life path number 2:

Most important for you right now is to learn the benefits of cooperation, patience and compromise. That means sometimes doing things that you find difficult, like listening when you would rather be talking. Once you have learned the importance of peacekeeping, you will discover that you have an ability to relate to others. You are a great person to have around if a fight is brewing. Just remember not to ignore your own needs while you make sure everyone else is working together.

Ideal study and career options for you are ones that allow you to negotiate, mediate, support, gather information, use your sensitivity and take care of important details. These skills

71

open the doors to a wide variety of professions, including health, law, business, teaching and art.

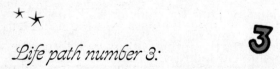

Life path number 3:

Your task right now is to learn to be both creative and spontaneous and to live your life with joy and imagination. Once you know how to express your emotions and enthusiasm you are ready to move on to the next phase – inspiring others.

You are a born communicator, and your wit and joyfulness will help others feel more optimistic about any situation. With 3 as your life path number you are creative and articulate, and you'll do well in anything artistic, be it writing, designing, illustration, dancing, singing or acting. You'll also suit any job where feelings and emotions are valued, such as public relations or customer service.

Life path number 4:

Right now you should concentrate on working hard and being reliable. Once you have mastered that you are ready to move take the next step – building for the future. Others look to people with life path 4 numbers to manage, control and make sure that everything runs smoothly. Have you already found yourself in this position at school or at home? Your friends look to you to organize party invites, or your younger sister expects you to remind her when her homework is due in.

With a 4 life path number you could shine in any managerial position or as an accountant, librarian or architect. You'll enjoy any job in which organization is valued, be it education, administration, politics or business. Your success will be in work that requires building things of lasting value.

Life path number 5:

At the moment you need to learn that change isn't something to be feared but a natural part of life. It is only through change that we learn and grow as people, and once you accept this you'll be ready to move to the next stage – enterprise and freedom.

With a 5 life path number you probably believe in freedom of all things, and you'll excel in any study or work that calls for energy and variety rather than routine. You won't enjoy a nine-to-five kind of job, and your best career options are ones that involve lots of change and diversity, such as working with the public, communications, advertising, publicity, sales, promotion, entertainment or journalism. A job that involves travel is also well suited to you.

⋆ ⋆

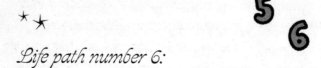

Life path number 6:

You should concentrate on helping and supporting others without neglecting yourself. Once you have accomplished this you will be able to move on to the next phase – balancing giving and receiving. With a 6 life path number you are one of life's givers and a born counseller. You are sympathetic and caring, and you may have found already that your friends turn to you first when they need support and advice.

What are the best options for you? You'll probably love any job in the service industry in which you can make life easier or more beautiful for others. Medicine, healthcare, counselling, teaching, gardening, decorating, training animals, beauty products, therapist of some kind, or a home-based business are all naturals for you.

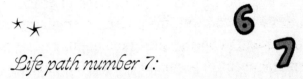

*⋆

Life path number 7:

Right now your priority is exploring the mysteries of the universe. You probably love reading and enjoy studying and analysing everything and everyone. Once you have understood that you are a born seeker of knowledge it's time for you to progress to the next stage – sharing your wisdom and insight with others. You may already have found that others seek you out for your wisdom or for help with homework.

People with life path number 7 are often teachers or academics, specializing in something quite specific, and this specialization puts them ahead of the game. Any job that calls for careful analysis, reasoning, scientific knowledge or technical ability would suit you perfectly. In addition, any field that allows you to study, contemplate or seek knowledge fits you well, such as a scientist, astronaut, researcher, writer or psychologist.

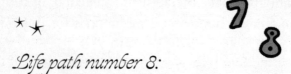

Life path number 8:

You will gradually learn that having money and material things does not always equal happiness. Once you've realized this you can move to the next level – being in charge.

Number 8s, like number 1s, are born leaders. They thrive in large businesses or organizations since power, authority and good judgement come naturally to them. If you have a number 8 life path number any field in which you can be in charge – be it chief financial officer, chief administrator, financial advisor, judge, president of a bank or even film director – is perfect for you.

76

Life path number 9:

Right now your mission is to learn
compassion and tolerance for all things. You may
already find that you have been touched by this
and have been involved in humanitarian activities,
such as campaigns for human or animal rights.
Once you learn this you can move to the next
stage – the importance of caring for each other.

Life path number 9s make born healers, but
your healing gift may come in a variety of forms,
such as writing, painting, dancing or counselling.
Study or work options well suited to you are the
arts, education, health or any line of work that is
designed to cure, help and humanize.

Money

Numerology won't necessarily help you win the
lottery, but if you are having trouble with money,
numerology can certainly help. Remind yourself of

your life path number, and check out this quick-fix advice to help you get back on track.

1: Try spending less on things you don't really need.

2: Well done! You are probably good at making ends meet, planning ahead and saving for rainy days. You deserve the odd treat though, so don't be afraid to splash out sometimes.

3: Debt may be a problem. While this is likely to pan out in the long term because of your potential to make lots of money, a little short-term prudence may be in order.

4: Although your easygoing attitude to money frees you from stress, a little forward planning wouldn't go amiss.

5: Your demanding social life takes its toll on your finances, but you are resourceful and hardworking and can always find ways to stay in the black.

6: Usually responsible and practical with cash, you are sometimes subject to massive retail binges. Try to restrain yourself for more long-term security.

7: You tend to be overcautious with your finances, which is a good thing, but be careful not to become miserly.

8: Big dreams often need big funds, so be careful to put away money to finance your long-term goals.

9: Red is the colour as far as your finances are concerned. You need to get a grip on your purse strings if you are to realize your hopes and dreams.

Numbers 4 and 8 are often considered good money numbers, and if they appear in your numerology readings you may well find that you have a knack for making and keeping money. Number 1 bodes well for new enterprises, numbers 2 and 6 for partnerships, number 7 for paying more attention to detail (it's also a great number for anything to do with school and study), and numbers 3, 5 and 9 suggest uncertainty, perhaps debt, if extravagance isn't checked. It might be wise to pay attention whenever these numbers appear in connection with money transactions as they suggest the need to organize, tend to business and take charge of your finances.

Lucky numbers

When asked to select a number between one and ten, more people will choose an odd number than an even. And most people will choose either a 3 or a 7. Now that you are studying numerology and becoming more familiar with the personalities of each number, can you understand why? It's not because they are luckier; it's simply because both 3 and 7 are associated with creative expression, imagination and wisdom.

123
456
789

Thirteen – unlucky or lucky?

Since ancient times 13 has received a really bad press, and the mistrust of the number still exists today. Hotels skip the 13th floor, and many airlines delete the 13th row from planes. The number 13 is also considered an unlucky number of guests at dinner parties. But 13 hasn't always been thought of as unlucky. The Aztecs thought that 13 had a mystical significance, and the United States shows no fear of the jinx. On the great seal of the US flag there are 13 stars, 13 stripes and an eagle with 13 features in each wing. The historian Ripley once constructed a list for Friday the 13th to show how lucky a date it actually was. So you see, there is no need to fear 13. It's just a number. Reduce it to 4, and you'll see that it, like every other number, has plenty of positive qualities.

What's your favourite number? As you have seen so far in this book, no number, including a 3 and a 7, is more or less lucky than another. Every number has an upside and a downside. The way for you to improve your luck is to maximize the positive potential and minimize the negative of

the number your intuition wants you to pay
attention to. Having a lucky number that keeps
springing to mind can come in very handy, not
for gambling or financial gain but for what that
number is trying to tell you. Have a look at the
sections in this book that refer to your lucky
number – or any number that you feel drawn to
at any time for no particular reason. As always
don't follow any significant number slavishly but
do think about how it can help you improve your
chances in luck and life.

CHAPTER SEVEN

Dreams

As you start using numbers in your everyday life and pay attention to their hidden meanings, you will find that they crop up more and more in your dreams. When this happens, your mind is using a particular number or combination of numbers to send you a message.

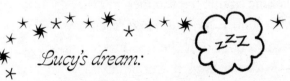

Lucy's dream:

Lucy's ambition was to go to university to study to become a journalist. To earn a place she needed respectable grades in English, maths, science and foreign languages. Science and maths came easy to her, and languages were no problem but she was struggling with

English. She was extremely upset when she failed her mock in English and even started to have nightmares. Her mum was worried and suggested finding her a personal tutor. It only took five lessons for Lucy to see that she was making progress, but the real breakthrough came after the second week, when she had a dream that boosted her confidence. In the dream she was sitting in her classroom at school struggling to write an essay. Every time she tried to write something she scribbled it out and started again. Just then she heard a clock strike four times. Suddenly the words flowed and she had no problem writing her essay.

Dreaming about the number 4 – the number of hard work, order and discipline – confirmed to Lucy that she was making good progress with her English and her extra lessons were helping her make sense of it all. Now she felt more confident – all the old doubts had disappeared.

Of course, many of us hope we'll dream of winning lottery numbers (and some people do!) but often dreams are not so easy to interpret. They may appear confusing because the information in them is presented in images and symbols. Just think of it as a form of shorthand your mind uses to tell you something. The images that appear in your dreams are your own thoughts and feelings turned into a series of pictures. For example, if you feel confused, you may dream of being lost in a wood. When a number appears in a dream, the message of that number will be found in the meanings that you associate with that number. This applies not only to numbers that you dream about but also to favourite numbers or numbers that simply come to mind for no reason in your waking life.

So what exactly do the numbers in your dreams or your daydreams mean? We'll take a look at them, one at a time. Don't forget, though, to pay attention to the unique details and context in which the numbers appear. Do you have happy or confusing feelings in your dream? This is important as it can help you find out whether your dream is a warning or an encouraging sign.

What does your mind want you to observe, feel, and think about? What is it trying to draw your attention to?

 1

In a dream the number 1 can refer to your being number one. Do you need to establish your identity in waking life? Perhaps you need to find your individuality and distinguish yourself from the crowd. Perhaps you should stand up for yourself or for what you believe in. Your dream could be encouraging you to become more independent. Alternatively, it could signify a new beginning or success, the promise of something new and the magic of new possibilities. It may also be a warning against being selfish or pushy.

 2

In a dream the number 2 symbolizes relationships, both romantic ones and friendships. It's the sign of a twosome – with a boyfriend or with a close friend. It can also suggest the desire for a special relationship or the need for balance. Is there a relationship in your life that needs to be kept in balance with equal give and take? Are you giving too much or taking too much? Dreaming about the number 2 may also mean that you need to put yourself in someone else's shoes or see an alternative point of view before making any important decisions.

The number 3 is a symbol of creativity, happiness, and joy and reflects the need to express what is true in your heart. In a dream it refers to your talents, style and self-expression. The number 3 encourages you to develop your creativity, but it is also the number of fun so it could be a sign of good things coming your way. In fairy tales there are always three wishes. Perhaps it is time for you to make yours!

In a dream the number 4 is linked to practical matters, hard work, a need for order, self-discipline and focus. To dream of this number may be a reminder that there is work for you to do or that you have duties to fulfil. If you feel positive when you dream about the number 4, your dream is telling you that you can achieve great things if you get organized and get on with your work.

 5

In a dream the number 5 represents adventure. Dreaming of this number suggests you might try something new or consider other options in your waking life. Perhaps it is time to be more alert, adventurous, sharp and experimental. If this number appears in your dreams your mind may be saying, 'Go on, explore, take a risk, have a go – you have nothing to lose but your fear!'

 6

The number 6 represents harmony, wisdom and knowledge. It is also the number of honesty and sincerity, so it could be pointing to someone who is sincere and genuine in your life. This is a person you can trust with your secrets and who will give you advice if you have a problem. Alternatively, your dream may be suggesting that there is a need for more honesty in your life. Perhaps you should look for harmony and balance in your life style or take better care of yourself.

 7

The number 7 is associated with music, art and literature, and when it appears in a dream it could be an encouragement to develop your skills and talents in these fields. Alternatively, if in real life you tend to be a bit of a daydreamer, this number may be telling you to be more practical and down-to-earth. Perhaps you need to spend less time alone and more with other people.

 8

Just by writing down the number 8, you can feel its continuous flow, so in dreams it might be telling you to relax a little and go with the flow. You could be in a lucky phase in which everything is going well. The number 8 is often connected with material wealth and riches, so to see this number in your dream could be a sign that good fortune is coming your way.

 9

The number 9 is associated with caring, sharing and giving. So to see it in a dream might mean either that you will be helping someone out or that someone will be helping you. Nine is also the number of unselfishness, so if you dream of number 9 you are probably a kind and thoughtful person. If you know that you are not, then your dream is telling you to learn a little kindness.

There is an ancient mystery and magic behind both dreams and numbers, so when you dream about numbers, a unique and very special message is being given to you. Pay attention to it. Search deep within your heart to decipher the meaning of that message. Learn the language of numbers in your dreams, and let them help you live your waking life to your fullest potential.

CHAPTER EIGHT

Your future

If only I had the power to see into the future and knew what it would take to be a success. Now that would be cool, wouldn't it?

Stella, 14

If I told you that by living a certain way you were guaranteed a happier outcome, wouldn't you want to know how? Well, you can do it! Just start with your destiny number. Your destiny number describes your purpose in life - your mission - and what you must do to feel most fulfilled. Although closely related to your life path number in the last chapter, it isn't the same. Your life path number indicates the skills that you have which can help you reach your destiny. Your destiny number reveals what will make you feel really satisfied.

Your name carries an energy pattern that spells out to the universe your direction in life, and it's from your birth name that you can find your destiny number. In other words, the numbers of your birth name indicate what you are destined for and the direction in which you will find your happiness. It's your cosmic code for success.

Finding out that my destiny number was a 3 really helped me in my decision to go for teacher training. I wasn't sure, but now I know that my destiny is to inspire and encourage. I haven't any doubts any more.

Simran, 17

I've always wanted to be a scientist but didn't think I'd be good enough. Being a 7 destiny number has really got me thinking that I have the ability to make a go of this.

Lisa, 14

Finding your destiny number

When figuring out your destiny number, you need to use your original name and all the names you were given at birth. Sorry, no nicknames or shortened versions of names. Whatever is on your birth certificate is the name to use, even if you hate or hide it. Every letter of every name counts!

NB If you were adopted and given a new name, or if you were given another name through your parents' remarrying and you know your original name, use your original name to work out your destiny number, as it represents your true essence. If you don't know your original name you will be working with the type of influence your adopted or new name is bringing into your life.

To find out your destiny number, write out your full name and then give each letter a number from the following chart.

A	1	J	1	S	1
B	2	K	2	T	2
C	3	L	3	U	3
D	4	M	4	V	4
E	5	N	5	W	5
F	6	O	6	X	6
G	7	P	7	Y	7
H	8	Q	8	Z	8
I	9	R	9		

Now add up each name separately, and then add the reduced numbers together to form a single digit.

For example:
Mary Jones:
4(M) + 1(A) + 9(R) + 7(Y) = 21; 2 + 1= 3
1(J) + 6(O) + 5(N) + 5(E) + 1(S) = 18; 1 + 8 = 9
3 + 9 = 12 and 1 + 2 = 3

Mary Jones's destiny number is 3.

Are you ready to meet your destiny?

Destiny number 1:

You are destined to be a leader. So go out and inspire others.

Generally confident and outgoing, you are a trendsetter with big dreams. The only things standing in your way are indecision, lack of concentration and overspending. Your mission in life is to be confident and original and to develop a sense of self rather than follow the lead of others. It's crucial for you to learn to stand alone, think alone and be an individual.

Typical 1: Liz Hurley

Destiny number 2:

You are destined to be a peacemaker. So embrace it and teach others to share.

A natural communicator, you are diplomatic, sensitive and thoughtful. To achieve your full potential you need to learn to invest as much effort into personal goals as in the happiness of those nearest to you. You can afford to be more demanding to ensure your own fulfilment. Work that allows you to develop other people's potential is most satisfying. Your purpose is to be adaptable, to create harmony and to find balance and cooperation.

Typical 2: Kylie Minogue

Destiny number 3:

You are destined to express yourself. So express yourself, and encourage others to do the same.

Experimental, dynamic and just a little frenetic, you're a natural-born leader. Whatever you choose to do in life, it's guaranteed that you'll speed along. Don't be too hasty though, it's important to enjoy the present moment too. Your mission in life is to inspire and encourage others with your enthusiasm. 'Bigger, better, faster' is your motto, but remember that the greatest pleasures come from little things. Take time to relax and enjoy your efforts.

Typical 3: Kim Cattrall

Destiny number 4:

Your destiny is to manage and organize. So create firm foundations and build on them.

A happy home and heart are crucial to you, and once you have these, the foundations are in place for you to make a success of yourself in any field you choose. You are demonstrative and romantic, and your destiny lies in your own hands. Your mission in life is to build something of lasting value, to be practical and work hard, to manage others and assure security for yourself and your friends.

Typical 4: Kate Winslet

Destiny number 5:

Your destiny is liberation and freedom. So embrace change and move forward.

You are feisty and passionate, and your natural dynamism means you are never far from the action. Search for the odd moment of calm to meditate on important things. You are ambitious and motivated, best suited to management roles or running your own business. Your vocation in life is to learn to adapt, change and progress. Your purpose is to allow yourself to be a free spirit and follow your curiosity wherever it leads you.

Typical 5: Victoria Beckham

Destiny number 6:

You are destined for nurturing. So help others, but don't neglect yourself.

Emotional and supportive, you gain most pleasure through close relationships. Your goal is to make your own needs a priority and not feel guilty. You excel in roles where you can help others achieve their full potential. Your mission in life is to serve, nurture and use your love of beauty and harmony to comfort and inspire.

Typical 6: Cate Blanchett

Destiny number 7:

You are destined to educate. So teach your wisdom.

Independent and self-motivated, you find that personal space and time are important. But beware that too much self-analysis can get in the way of your progress. Teamwork intimidates you, and you prefer to get jobs done under your own steam. To succeed you must banish the self-doubt that plagues you. Your mission in life is to analyse and seek out. Your purpose is to dig deep, find your inner wisdom and pass on your knowledge.

Typical 7: Geri Halliwell

Destiny number 8:

You are destined to achieve material success. So get out there and be the powerful leader you were born to be.

Your ambitions are sky-high, and your confidence will take you most of the way, whichever direction you choose. Just be sure to select one that allows you to direct your energies wisely. Your mission is to understand yourself, and your purpose is to achieve and succeed using your visionary skill at organization.

Typical 8: Naomi Campbell

Destiny number 9:

You are destined to love. So reach out and help others.

With your sunny disposition, you want the whole world to smile with you. It often does, but a little practicality will help you balance reality with your dreams. You are excellent at outside-the-box, big-picture creative thinking, but you need to work on developing the practical skills to make it happen in the real world. You have great vision and humanitarian dreams of changing the world for the better, and with a little more pragmatic thinking you can make an impact. Your mission is to love unconditionally, and your purpose is to strive for universal fellowship using your selflessness, sensitivity and healing art.

Typical 9: Gwyneth Paltrow

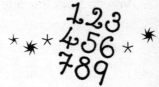

IT'S YOUR NUMBER - OWN IT!

It's pointless to start wishing you have a different number because each of the numbers can lead to success and point the way to your purpose in life. If you are having a tough time perhaps the challenging aspects of that number are coming to the fore. Hang in there, work on the strengths of your number and see what happens.

*⅄ THE BIGGER PICTURE

Now that you have figured out your birthday,
personality, soul, life path and destiny numbers,
write them all down and take a look at the bigger
picture. What are your strengths? How can you
build on them? What qualities and or numbers are
missing from the picture? What does that teach
you about yourself? Remember the whole purpose
of numerology is to give you an insight into who
YOU are and help put you on a path that's right
for you. Do keep a sense of perspective though
and never forget that other things such as your
common sense and your intuition are just as
important.

CHAPTER NINE

Names, numbers and YOU again

Are you getting more familiar with the numbers in your life? If you've been working out your numbers, and perhaps even the numbers of your boyfriend, family and friends, the traits and trends associated with each number should start to become easier to recognize. You may even feel that each number has a personality of its own: the pioneering 1 who loves to take the lead, the peace-loving and supportive number 2, the enthusiastic and inspiring number 3, the disciplined and hardworking 4, the charismatic and free-spirited number 5, the nurturing and responsible 6, the wise and mysterious 7, the powerful and authoritative 8 and the visionary and tolerant 9.

When you start to feel comfortable and familiar with numbers you can really start to have fun with them in your daily life. We've already introduced you to your phone number, money numbers, dream numbers, lucky numbers and house numbers, and in this final chapter let's think once again about something you hear and use every day but may not pay that much attention to - your name.

What's in a name?

Have you ever met someone and their name seems just right or completely wrong for them? When it comes to names, numerology can reveal a lot, and we touched on this earlier when we figured out your soul, personality and destiny numbers. But it doesn't stop there. Each part of your name reveals information about you.

⋆ **123 456 789** *⋆

*⋏ YOUR FIRST NAME

Referring to the letters and numbers chart on page 94, add up the numbers in your first name, both consonants and vowels, and reduce to a single digit. This number is called your growth or challenge number, and it shows what you need to do to develop your full potential. For example, if your growth number is 3, self-expression, creativity, and inspiring others are ways for you to move forward with your life.

It doesn't stop there. The first vowel in your first name reveals the way you could approach life to maximize your chances of success. What's the first vowel in your name?

A = 1   The focus is on leadership and
individuality.

E = 5   The focus is on curiosity and
investigation.

I = 9   The focus is on intuition and
humanitarianism.

O = 6   The focus is on responsibility and family.

U = 3   The focus is on creativity and enthusiasm.

✴⋏ YOUR MIDDLE NAME

Your middle name is thought to reveal your
emotional life, your likes and dislikes and your
marriage suitability. Write out your middle name,
and add up all the numbers until they become a
single digit. If you have two middle names, treat
them as one and count up all the letters in the
names and reduce to one digit. If you don't have
a middle name, look to your last name.

★⅄ YOUR LAST NAME

Just as we inherit genetic characteristics, like eye colour and height, we also inherit subtle traits through our family name. Your inherited traits are calculated by working with your last name at birth. Here's a quick reference for checking out what your family name number means:

1. You have inherited an independent spirit, a strong will and an ability to think up original ideas.

2. You have inherited a peaceful and loving nature and the desire to reduce conflict.

3. You have inherited an outgoing, optimistic personality, a great sense of humour and a creative spirit.

4. You have inherited a sense of self-discipline and the importance of hard work to get what you want.

5. You have inherited a belief that you are a free spirit. Change is easy for you, and you are a risk taker.

6. You have inherited a conservative, family-oriented approach to life and a sense of responsibility towards others.

7. You have inherited a desire for learning. Your family traits are observation, analysis and a need for privacy.

8. You have inherited an ambitious attitude towards money and power. Your family name brings you the qualities of leadership and organization.

9. You have inherited a compassionate and sympathetic nature as well as a sense of needing to serve others.

In numerology we look at adopted names or married names as additional influences. Your original birth name is the most significant name because it tells you the essence of who you are, but if you don't know your birth name your present name is still crucial. Your current name represents the influences you are presently living under and the strengths and weaknesses that are accompanying you through life, right now.

*⅄ CHOOSING A NAME

If you don't like your birth name, you may be thinking of changing it. Remember, though, that your birth name is your destiny, and you never lose this cosmic code. A new name can enhance your original name energy, but it can't replace it – you will just have two sets of numbers operating simultaneously. If you are considering a name change, be absolutely sure you understand your birth name well before you give it up. You need to know who you are before you try to be someone else.

A new name or nickname will not guarantee success or change your life. The only thing that will change your life is the way YOU choose to work with the energies of the numbers associated with your name. When choosing a name of any kind, choose one that you find inspiring and that feels comfortable to use. Take your time to think about what your new name means and what kind of power it will bring into your life. And bear in mind that it takes about five years before its energy is fully integrated.

Adding it all up

In this book I've tried to show how you can lead a happy, successful and harmonious life by knowing what your numbers reveal about you and the world you live in. The rest is up to you. Every number carries within it the seeds of happiness, success and fulfilment. Trust your instincts, use your common sense and always remember that you make your decisions and not the numbers. You were born with everything you need to succeed. Numerology proves that you don't have to look anywhere else.

Whether you think numerology is a true science or just a fun thing to do, you can't avoid being impressed by what your numbers bring to light. In your everyday life you can refer to it over and over again to decode hidden meanings and discover your own special magic powers. If you think positively and you are energetic and persistent, it's amazing what you can accomplish.

Index